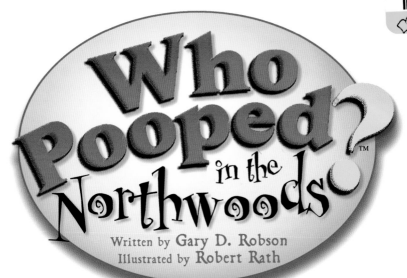

Who Pooped? in the Northwoods

Written by Gary D. Robson

Illustrated by Robert Rath

FARCOUNTRY
PRESS

To Gary Ferguson:
Thanks for your help, encouragement, and inspiration.
- Gary

For Lucy and Thomas, my poop experts.
- Robert

ISBN: 978-1-56037-434-3

For more information on our books,
write Farcountry Press, P.O. Box 5630, Helena, MT 59604;
call (800) 821-3874; or visit www.farcountrypress.com.

Manufactured by
Versa Press, Inc.
Spring Bay Road / Route 26
East Peoria, IL 61611-9788
in February 2015

Book design by Robert Rath.

 Produced and printed in the United States of America.

19 18 17 16 15   3 4 5 6 7

Library of Congress Cataloging-in-Publication Data

Robson, Gary D.
Who pooped in the North Woods? / written by Gary D. Robson ; Illustrated by Robert Rath.
p. cm.
ISBN 13: 978-1-56037-434-3 (softcover)
ISBN 10: 1-56037-434-9 (softcover)
1. Animal tracks--Northeastern States--Juvenile literature.
2. Tracking and trailing--Northeastern States--Juvenile literature. I. Title.
QL768.R594 2008
591.47'9--dc22
2007037892

"Are we there yet?" Michael said as he squirmed in the back seat. "I have to go to the bathroom."

"We're already in the Northwoods," said Dad. "But hang on, Michael, we'll be at our campsite pretty soon."

NORTHWOODS

MINNESOTA WISCONSIN MICHIGAN

"There are a lot of places here to stop and hike," said Mom. "Why don't we go for a walk after lunch?"

"Michael's too scared to hike," said Emily. "He thinks a bear's gonna get him." She curved her fingers like claws and snarled at Michael.

4

"Stop it, Emily," said Mom. "Nobody's getting eaten by anything."

Michael was excited about the trip, but Emily was right. He had just read a book about Northwoods bears, and they were scary!

"I *am* kind of scared of bears," admitted Michael.

"Don't worry," Dad told him. "Bears are scared of people, too. We probably won't even see one."

"Besides," Mom added, "we're going to show you how to count a bear's toes without ever getting close to one."

Once they unpacked and set up their tents, the family was ready to hit the trail.

Dad said, "Let's look for some animal *sign*, and we'll show you what Mom was talking about."

"Sign?" said Michael, puzzled. "You mean like a sign at the zoo?"

BARRED OWL

MOOSE

WOLF

Dad smiled. "A 'sign' is a clue an animal has left behind," he said. "It tells us where an animal has been and what it's been doing."

"Like these chewed-down trees?" said Emily.

"Exactly," said Dad. "That's a sign that beavers are in the area."

the STRAIGHT POOP

Beavers gnaw on wood to sharpen their teeth.

"Here's another clue!" Michael shouted. "Footprints!"

"Good eyes!" said Mom. "Those are beaver tracks. See how the back feet are webbed? Webbed feet help the beavers swim."

"And here's some beaver scat," Dad said, pointing to something lumpy, bumpy, and brown.

"*Scat?*" asked Emily. "What's scat?"

"Scat is a word hikers and trackers use for animal poop," Dad replied.

the STRAIGHT POOP

Beavers eat tree bark and use branches to build their dams and lodges.

"Normally, beavers poop in the water or in their dens," Dad continued. "We're lucky to see beaver scat."

"*Lucky?*" said Emily. "Lucky to see *poop*?"

"I think it's cool!" Michael said.

"I found scat from a really big rabbit," said Michael, trying to sound grown up. "Bigger than my rabbit, Fluffy."

As they walked down the trail, the kids darted around, very excited about looking for animal sign.

"It looks a little like rabbit scat," said Dad, "But it's actually from a deer."

"How can you tell?" Emily asked.

"Rabbit scat is small and round, like little balls," Mom explained. "Deer scat is shaped more like jellybeans."

DEER SCAT

RABBIT SCAT

the STRAIGHT POOP

Deer scat looks different in the springtime, when they are eating fresh, rich new leaves.

SPRING SCAT

WINTER SCAT

JELLYBEANS

"And here's an antler!" Michael said, touching the white points of the antler. "Did a bear eat the deer?"

"I don't think so," Dad said. "Deer lose their antlers every year and grow new, bigger ones. The antlers that fall off are called 'sheds.'"

the STRAIGHT POOP

Horns are not the same as antlers. Antlers are shaped like branches and fall off every year. Horns do not fall off and continue growing over an animal's lifetime.

"Are these deer tracks over here?" asked Emily.

"Good eye!" said Mom. "See how the tracks are split down the middle? Deer hooves have two parts."

the STRAIGHT
POOP

Look for deer sign on the trees. Deer often rub their antlers on trees, removing some of the bark.

WALKING

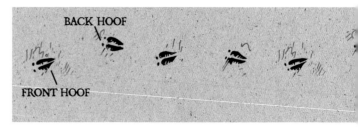

BACK HOOF

FRONT HOOF

"This deer was in a hurry," said Mom, as she studied the ground.

Michael and Emily went over to look.

"How can you tell?" asked Emily. She was having fun figuring out the clues that the animals left behind.

"See how the hoofprints get very far apart here," Mom explained, "and the front prints are behind the back prints?"

RUNNING

PRONKING

the STRAIGHT POOP

Sometimes mule deer bounce along with all four feet hitting the ground together. This is called "stotting" or "pronking."

FRONT HOOVES

BACK HOOVES

BACK HOOVES

FRONT HOOVES

"Was the deer walking backwards?" said Emily.

"No, it was galloping. Something scared it and it was moving fast," Dad said.

DEER LEG 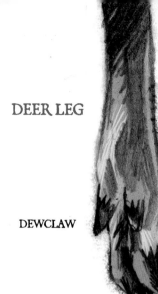 DOG LEG 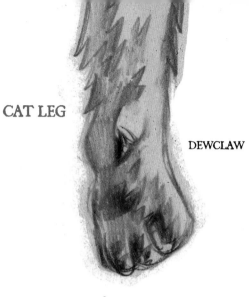 CAT LEG

DEWCLAW

DEWCLAW

DEWCLAW

"What are these little marks?" asked Emily, pointing to two little dents behind each track.

"Those are from the deer's *dewclaws*," said Mom.

Emily thought Mom was teasing her. "Deer don't have claws!" Emily cried.

"Dewclaws are small claws partway up an animal's legs," Mom explained. "Lots of animals have them, including dogs and cats."

"Here's what scared the deer," said Dad. "There are wolf tracks and scat all around here."

The family rushed over to look.

"They look like big dog tracks," said Michael.

"That's because wolves are members of the dog family," said Dad.

"Wolf scat also looks like dog poop, except that it has bits of bones and hair in it," Mom added.

"Yuck!" said Emily.

the STRAIGHT POOP

Scientists study what wolves eat by examining wolf scat.

19

"Are there a lot of wolves around the Northwoods?" asked Michael, looking anxiously around him.

"There used to be thousands," Mom said. "But when I was a little girl, there were no wolves left in Wisconsin, Minnesota, and Michigan, except for a few hundred in northern Wisconsin and Michigan's Upper Peninsula."

the STRAIGHT POOP

The states of Michigan, Minnesota, and Wisconsin paid bounties to anyone killing wolves in the early 1900s. The states stopped paying bounties by 1960, and wolf populations have been increasing ever since.

"They're coming back though," said Dad. "All three states are working to protect the wolves and bring them back into their old territory."

"This probably comes from a snowshoe hare," Dad said. "Hares are bigger than the cottontail rabbits, and their poop is bigger, too."

"Here's the rabbit scat you were looking for," said Dad.

"Yeah," said Emily, "but it's a lot bigger than Fluffy's."

the STRAIGHT POOP

Rabbits eat their own poop! They do this to get as much nutrition from the food as they can. The little brown balls are scat that's been through the rabbit twice.

SNOWSHOE HARE IN WINTER

the STRAIGHT POOP

Snowshoe hares change color with the seasons. In the summer, they're gray or brown. In the winter, they turn white.

SNOWSHOE HARE IN SUMMER

FRONT
TRACKS

BACK
TRACKS

**SNOWSHOE HARE
TRACKS**

"You need to find the tracks to identify what kind of rabbit or hare it is," Mom said. "Snowshoe hare tracks are bigger and wider than cottontail rabbit tracks."

the STRAIGHT POOP

Hares are related to rabbits, but they are not the same.

SNOWSHOE HARE   COTTONTAIL RABBIT

FRONT TRACKS

BACK TRACKS

**COTTONTAIL
RABBIT
TRACKS**

"I think I found a baby wolf footprint!" yelled Emily.

"You know what you found?" asked Mom. "Bobcat tracks. A bobcat track has four toes like a wolf track, but there are no claw marks. Also the front of the big pad looks dented in."

"And see here?" Dad said. "One toe sticks out farther in front than the others."

the STRAIGHT
POOP

Bobcats may be big wild cats, but they still bury their scat just like a housecat.

"*Bob*-cat?" Michael asked.
"Why not a *Michael*-cat?"

"It's called a bobcat because of its short bobbed tail," smiled Dad. "There's a less common short-tailed cat called a lynx that also lives in the Northwoods."

BOBBED TAIL

LONG
TAIL

BOBCAT

HOUSE
CAT

CLAW
MARKS

BOBCAT
TRACKS

TOES
ARE EVEN

WOLF
TRACKS

the STRAIGHT POOP

Cats can retract their claws, so their tracks don't show claw marks.

All dogs, except grey foxes, leave tracks with claw marks.

"What's *this* funny-looking poop?" Michael asked. He was getting very excited about all of the scat they were finding.

"Mi-chael, *that's* not poop," Emily chimed in. "That's an owl's cough pellet."

"A cough pellet?" said Michael. "Does it have a cold?

the STRAIGHT POOP

Studying owl pellets is a great way to find out what owls eat. Snowy owls dine on a wide variety of small animals, including mice, squirrels, birds, rabbits, and hares.

"Owls eat their prey whole," explained Dad. "The parts they can't digest, like hair and bones, they cough up in pellets like this."

"Yuck!" said Michael.

"There's more owl sign over here," said Dad. "See these tracks with two toes pointing forward and two back, and the owl poop streaked down the side of the tree?"

the STRAIGHT POOP

Owls see very well at night, but they aren't blind during the day. Owls even hunt during the day.

"Check out these owl tracks," said Emily from farther down the trail. "They're *gigantic*!"

Mom hurried over. "They're wild turkey tracks," she said. "See the tracks are larger and have three toes."

the STRAIGHT POOP

Benjamin Franklin wanted to make the wild turkey the American national bird instead of the bald eagle.

"Barred owls are big," said Dad.
"But turkeys are bigger—their wingspan can be longer than my arms."

33

Emily knelt down to peer at
some tiny tracks near a puddle.

"Look at these teeny tracks,"
she said. "Are they from
a mouse?"

"No, they're from a short-tailed weasel, which is also called an ermine," Mom said. "Weasels may be tiny, but they're great hunters."

the STRAIGHT POOP

Weasels have five toes on each foot. Rodents, such as mice and squirrels, have five toes on the back feet and only four toes on the front feet.

"Here's more deer tracks and scat," said Michael. "This must be a *huge* deer!"

"You found moose sign!" said Dad. "Moose scat and tracks are bigger than a deer's because the moose is so much bigger. They are called the giants of the Northwoods."

"Moose may look big and awkward," said Mom, "but they can actually move very quietly through the forest, even with those large antlers."

"Did the moose do this to the tree with his antlers?" asked Michael.

"It looks like something was sharpening its claws, Michael," said Mom. "And see how high those scratch marks go? That animal was pretty big."

"It's not just the animal that's big," said Emily. "Check out the size of this poop!"

"It looks like we've found Michael's black bear," said Dad.

"Let's see what you learned today," said Mom. "What can you figure out about this bear?"

"I'd say the bear is as tall as Dad, and has really long claws," said Michael slowly.

the STRAIGHT POOP

Black bears eat almost anything. They live on berries, honey, leaves, nuts, twigs, and insects, but they also hunt small animals and fish.

"I'd say it's been eating plants," said Emily, "because there aren't any hairs or bones in its poop."

"Good!" said Mom. "What else?"

"Look at this footprint," said Michael. "The track is really big and has five toes like a short-tailed weasel's, instead of four toes like a bobcat's."

"I told you you'd be able to count a black bear's toes," laughed Dad.

Emily plucked some hairs from the tree trunk. "You said this was a black bear," said Emily. "But these hairs are reddish brown."

"Black bears can be black, brown, or cinnamon-colored, like this one," said Mom. "There are even black bears so light-colored they're almost white."

the STRAIGHT POOP

Bears like to scratch their backs on rough tree bark, and they often leave hairs behind.

As the family ate dinner that night, everyone talked about how much fun they were having in the Northwoods.

"We didn't see very many animals," said Emily, "but it seemed like we did!"

Everyone laughed
when Michael said,
"And I didn't get
scared once!"

45

SNOWSHOE HARE

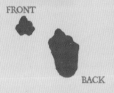

FRONT

BACK

Tracks are wider than rabbit tracks. Small tracks are filled in between toes.

Scat is in small, brown balls.

BEAVER

FRONT

BACK

Large tracks with slender toes. Drag marks from tail often blur or erase tracks.

Though rarely seen, scat is marshmallow-sized and filled with wood chips.

WHITE-TAILED DEER

Pointy, split-hoof tracks with curved sides.

Scat is oval-shaped like jellybeans.

MOOSE

Tracks are larger and less pointed than deer tracks.

Scat is larger and rounder than deer scat.

BLACK BEAR

FRONT

BACK

Large tracks with claws.

Scat changes depending on diet, but usually contains vegetation.

SCAT NOTES

WOLF

FRONT

BACK

NO DENT

Large dog-like tracks with claw marks visible.

Scat is dark, tapered, and contains hair.

BOBCAT

LEADING TOE

DENT

FRONT

BACK

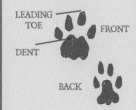

Tracks are smaller than a wolf's, but claws don't show.

Scat is rarely seen because they bury it.

SHORT-TAILED WEASEL

FRONT

BACK

Tiny tracks are dime-sized.

Scat is black, ropey, and often twisted.

BARRED OWL

Tracks show four toes: two toes pointing forward and two pointing backward or sideways.

Scat is runny and white. "Cough pellets" contain fur and bones.

WILD TURKEY

Tracks show three slender toes pointing forward, and one toe pointing backward. Occasionally the back toe doesn't show.

Long, narrow scat is brown in the middle and greenish-white on the ends.

ABOUT the AUTHOR and ILLUSTRATOR

GARY D. ROBSON lives in Montana, not too far from Yellowstone Park, where he and his wife own a bookstore and tea bar. Gary has written dozens of books and hundreds of articles, mostly related to science, nature, and technology.

www.GaryDRobson.com

ROBERT RATH is a book designer and illustrator living in Bozeman, Montana. Although he has worked with Scholastic Books, Lucasfilm, and The History Channel, his favorite project is keeping up with his family.

BOOKS IN THE
WHO POOPED IN THE PARK?
SERIES:

Olympic • • Glacier
• Cascades • Black Hills • Northwoods
Redwoods • Yellowstone • Ac
• Grand Teton

Yosemite • Rocky Mountain • Shenandoah •
Sequoia/ Red Rock
Kings • Canyon • Colorado Plateau
Canyon • Grand Canyon • Great Smoky Mountains
Death Valley • Sonoran Desert
• Big Bend